Cooperstown Verses

Cooperstown Verses

Poems About Each Hall of Famer

MARK W. SCHRAF

foreword by MIKE SHANNON

To JAKE AND APRIL,

FINALLY! EVEN THOUGH YOU
MIGHT NOT BE THE BIGGEST
BASEBALL FANS EVER, YOUR SUPPORT
MAKES ME FEEL LIKE YOU LOVE
BASEBALL POETRY! THANKS, AND
ENJOY!

LOVE,

mark

McFarland & Company, Inc., Publishers
Jefferson, North Carolina, and London

Library of Congress Cataloguing-in-Publication Data

Schraf, Mark W., 1963–
    Cooperstown verses : poems about each Hall of Famer /
Mark W. Schraf ; foreword by Mike Shannon.
       p.   cm.
    Includes index.
    ISBN 0-7864-1148-1 (softcover : 60# alkaline paper) ∞
    1. National Baseball Hall of Fame and Museum — Poetry.
2. Baseball players— Poetry.   3. Baseball — Poetry.   I. Title.
PS3619.C46C66   2001
811'.6 — dc21   2001126808

British Library cataloguing data are available

Manufactured in the United States of America

Cover image ©2001 Wood River Gallery.

McFarland & Company, Inc., Publishers
  Box 611, Jefferson, North Carolina 28640
    www.mcfarlandpub.com

For my wife,
who read just a few lines
yet loved every poem,
and for my granddad,
who always played catch with me for as long as I wanted.

Acknowledgments

The author wishes to thank the following publications and publishers where the following poems first appeared:

- "Why This Bleacher Bum Hates Ernie Banks," from *Baseball Stories for the Soul*; Madden Publishing Company;
- "All They Ever Wanted" and "21@65: '99" (published as 21@62: '96) from *I Saw Rod Scurry*; Polo Grounds Press;
- "Blue Blood," "The Devil in Veracruz," "The Good Fight," and "Kniekro," from *Spitball: The Literary Baseball Magazine*.

Contents

Foreword

BY MIKE SHANNON

Writing poetry (not to mention reading poetry) is one of mankind's purest activities. Nobody ever does it anymore (if they ever did) for the money. As for fame, well, the return on one's investment is a little better, but the truth is that writing a book of poetry probably confers a tad more fame than running as a third party presidential candidate, and certainly less than appearing as a castaway cast member on the inane TV show *Survivor*.

So the question arises, Why put oneself through the ordeal required to pen something poetically significant, when the same brain cells might be employed in machinations to improve the performance of one's mutual fund IRAs? Some may feel that the question goes double when the subject of the book is something traditionally supposed to be as unpoetic as baseball.

The answers to both questions are simple and heart-warming. Poets in general continue to do their thing in the absence of any expectation of being paid a sum of money anywhere close to matching the amount of work invested because the inexhaustible drive to create is fundamental to the human spirit. Baseball poets continue to step into the batter's box and take their cuts for the same reason other poets do but also because, believe it or not, there is a loyal audience, small though it may be, for baseball poetry.

Every baseball literature aficionado knows by now that the existence of this audience was first truly recognized in the early 1980s by several small press baseball magazines; *Spitball: The Literary Baseball Magazine* and *The Minneapolis Review of Baseball* (later renamed *Elysian Fields Quarterly*) were the first and the most important of these journals. A number of interesting chapbooks of baseball poetry were also published in the last two decades of the past century, including *I Saw Rod Scurry* (Polo Grounds Press, 1997), an eyebrow-raising debut of sorts for the baseball poet of the moment, Mr. Schraf, and a harbinger of greater things to come — namely, this book. Which leads us to the third, and unheralded arm of this movement, McFarland & Company, who published book-length collections of baseball poetry by some of the most prolific of contemporary baseball poets—Gene Fehler, Robert L. Harrison, and Gene Carney. These books have made vital contributions to baseball poetry in that it is necessary to read a substantial number of a poet's works to assess and appreciate his talent, and the encouragement that McFarland has given serious baseball poets cannot be overestimated. Appropriately, the company's efforts were recently recognized when Tim Peeler's *Touching All the Bases: Poems from Baseball* received a finalist's nomination in 2000 for that year's CASEY Award, the bronze plaque awarded annually since 1983 by *Spitball Magazine* to the author and publisher of the best baseball book of the year.

Of course, in the present case, with *Cooperstown Verses: Poems About Each Hall of Famer*, the poems, numerous though they be, most definitely needed to be published together, all at once, as they are not merely a collection of unrelated poems (or poems related only by the topic baseball) but an organic literary entity conceived as a single whole by the poet.

And what of that conception? Where would a man get an idea to write a poem about every member of the Baseball Hall of Fame? Other than a tavern where the liquor and baseball talk were flowing freely, I suppose one would most likely get such an idea in Cooperstown, New York, where the National Baseball Hall of Fame and Museum is located. I happen to know that Mr. Schraf has visited Cooperstown many times, because for more than a decade now he and I have made a pilgrimage there every summer to cover the annual Induction Day ceremonies for a variety of newspapers and magazines. While a visit to the Hall of Fame at any time of year is an intoxicating event for any baseball fan, being in Cooperstown during Induction Weekend is truly inspirational; and no matter how jaded we become, our annual visit to Cooperstown always rejuvenates our passion for the game.

Now, assuming Mr. Schraf's yearly visits to Cooperstown during the most magical season of the Hall of Fame calendar explains how he came up with his fantastic conceit, we are still tempted to query, What would possess a man to try to pull off such a feat! Well, at this point, dear friend, I am afraid we enter exotic, murky waters where only death-wishing daredevils, inveterate masochists, and madmen touched by genius dare to sail. I leave it to you to decide which of these three types (if not all three) best describes Mr. Schraf, but suffice it to say that he has returned from his adventure with a trove of poems as exotic and dazzling as ducats.

From the treacherous waters of verbosity and mangled metaphors, I'll return to the terra firma of simplicity and directness, pointing out that

Mr. Schraf faced a considerable, double-sided problem in undertaking the composition of *Cooperstown Verses*. On the one hand, he faced the challenge of avoiding cliché while writing about the greatest of baseball greats, about whom it is difficult to say anything new; and on the other, he was required to find something meaningful to say about those less well-known, those we might even paradoxically call "obscure" Hall of Famers, about whom it is difficult to say anything at all that is interesting, much less poetic. While it is not to be expected that every poem in a work as long as this would be equally successful, it is clear that Mr. Schraf has compiled a very high batting average indeed and produced a book worthy of his subjects. Surely, every reader will be struck by the variety of poetic forms, techniques, and voices employed here and by the considerable wit, intelligence, humor, baseball knowledge, and verbal ingenuity that is displayed on nearly every page.

Finally, while the Baseball Hall of Fame and Museum is a national treasure, it is not these historic and priceless artifacts which make it one of America's best-loved institutions, but the players, managers, umpires, and administrators who have been elected as members to the Hall of Fame proper, the most prestigious honorary sports club in the world. Members of the Baseball Hall of Fame are not as powerful as presidents of the United States, but they are more popular and more revered and have become, in fact, American royalty. *Cooperstown Verses* recognizes this elevation of the baseball Hall of Famer in the consciousness of our nation. Appreciative only of facts and statistics, many baseball fans unfortunately blind themselves to the insights and unproveable truths good poetry affords. Mr. Schraf's book may not be the last word on the members of the Baseball Hall of Fame in a factual sense, but it is a scrapbook of exciting new clippings that reveal in a poetic sense some wonderful things to us about these men, about baseball, and about the uses of poetry itself.

Preface

Cooperstown. The mere mention of the word evokes a myriad of images and emotions to even the most cavalier of baseball fans, and to those in love with the game, it is Mecca, its members deities. The fact that you're reading this introduction most likely places you firmly into the category of *Baseball Fan*, unless you're simply a *Poetry Fan*. In any case, this book is all about images and emotions, and I submit that the combination of poetry and baseball is especially well suited for exploring those two staples of human experience.

The concept for this project was simple: write a poem about everyone in the Hall of Fame. I decided early on to limit the scope of the book only to the elected members. While many think of Ernie Harwell and Bob Prince and Len Koppett and Ring Lardner as Hall of Famers, they really aren't. Their considerable contributions to the game have been recognized by the Ford Frick Award for excellence in sportswriting or the J.G. Taylor Spink Award for outstanding broadcast journalism. They deserve all accolades and every recognition, and perhaps someone even ought to write a poem about every last one of them, but they don't belong in this book. The guys with the plaques, the 253 men depicted in these poems, are the Hall of Fame, and they alone are the subject of *Cooperstown Verses*.

Once the question of *who* was decided, next up was the *how*. I knew that I wasn't interested in 200-odd hagiographic poems extolling stellar careers and saintly qualities, and I assumed you wouldn't be, either. And yes, I'm aware of my religious reference mere paragraphs before, and, as one who is without question smitten with baseball, I still believe it to be valid. However, a continual barrage of "He was the best" and "What a guy" and "Hall of Immortals" would have been monotonous, banal. Instead, I was much more interested in the unique perspective, the uncommon idea, the challenging treatment.

Some of the poems were taken directly from my experiences as a fan, either factual (Ralph Garr really did react in a game as he did in the Maze-roski poem) or pseudo-factual (I don't have a brother, but my first curse words were spewed violently toward the TV image of Johnny Bench after his Reds beat my Pirates in the 1972 Championship Series). Other players required some measure of research. For instance, who among us can extemporaneously recite five things about Jake Beckley, interesting or not? Three things? Additionally, with 250 poems to write, composing a series of 50 pages-long odes to George Kell and Ford Frick, while terribly unlikely in itself, would also lengthen the manuscript to unpublishable propor-tions. The goal was to find one thing, one image or emotion, one distinc-tive connection with each Hall of Famer.

So I read. And learned. And walked, sometimes for days and weeks at a time, with a picture of a player in front of my eyes, or the words of his obituary ringing in my ears. And I did not, would not, could not stop until I found one hook, at least one thing about him that I could trans-late, into poetry.

Many of the details in the poems may not be known to some read-ers. While my intention was not to publish a book of trivia poems, nor to boast vainly of scholarship, you may nevertheless need to do some inves-tigating of your own to determine what is fact and what is, well, poetry. *The Baseball Encyclopedia* (or the ever popular *Total Baseball*), combined with any good biographical reference like Mike Shatzkin's *The Ballplayers,* should present the stats, facts, and photography to grease the wheels of knowledge. I hope that reading some of these poems will inspire you to learn more about the men portrayed in this book.

Not every poem is flattering. If you happen to be a charter member of the Morgan Bulkeley Fan Club, please accept my apologies in advance and realize that these poems are not the only possible way to view each of the subjects. Quite often, a poem reflects not my opinion at all, but the imagined view of a player or fan. Indeed, just as there are many aspects to our own lives and personalities and experiences, so is it true for these men, perhaps even more so.

Certainly not every poem is serious, and some are actually quite silly. But one of baseball's greatest appeals is that its players look like they're having fun, and I feel certain that the poetry legitimately reflects that sense of frivolity. How do you think Rabbit Maranville got himself elected, any-way?

There are many different forms of poetry to be found in the book, from haiku to metered verse to prose poetry to limerick, with a few par-odies thrown in for seasoning. I hope the variety keeps the front-to-back reader from becoming bored with one style, and for those who pick out the poems of their favorite team's HOFers, I hope I didn't accidentally write 18 straight haiku about the White Sox.

All baseball fans should promise themselves a visit to the National Baseball Hall of Fame and Museum in Cooperstown. It's a special, magical place, and as you gaze in wonder at Ty Cobb's glove or Casey Stengel's flip-down sunglasses or George Brett's pine tar rag, what you see and feel will take root and remain in your memory for a lifetime. Memories like those inspired me to write these poems. And, who knows? By the time you finish "Robin Yount Was Never," you might just consider yourself a *Baseball Poetry Fan*.

— Mark Schraf

Not Hammer

No one wanted it to be you
Ted maybe, or Mickey yes
Mickey of course Mickey but
He pissed it all away or maybe
Even Willie sure Willie Say Hey
Missah Leo New York Willie
But not you
Night dark night quiet nightmare
For pitchers and reporters
Too colored with not
Enough color
You weren't even active like
Jackie just a sleepy-eyed pro
Everyday doing his job with
Casual brilliance hammering
At the records until they
Collapsed and you could finally say
You were glad it was over which
Was exactly what they hoped you
Wouldn't but knew you'd say and
Now you still feel like they don't
Want it to be you you may not be
Wrong

Had the Great Alexander
Lived to See His Own Movie

they yanked him from
some dive scrubbed him clean
dried him out perched him next
to Ronnie for the Hollywood Premier
but the truth remained
forever etched in the tired lines
and vacuous stare and ducking the
ovations as if they were line drives
back through the box he
muttered as he bobbed and weaved
to the next saloon where the hell was
my Doris Day

WALT ALSTON (1911–1984)   *inducted in 1983*

Smokey

Sandwiched between Durocher/Dressen and
Lasorda like a thick slab of Havarti aged
twenty-three years

Proving that sometimes

> doing nothing
> gets the job
> done

But did the W's ever erase the rancid
moldy aftertaste of your solitary

K

The Fairy Tale Denied

The season for romance : spring
and every year Sparky'd fall
for the prettiest young thing at
the dance.

Tell everyone who'd listen how
this one
    had it all
this one
    was gonna go all the way
this one
    was different from all
the others.

And when his fantasy date once again
turned hideous Sparky ever the blind
romantic would paint a smile on his craggy
old heart.

"Just a rough start" he'd whistle
through the graveyard until the
shards of slipper glass finally
poked too many gaping holes in
his lineup.

Never did learn you can't be
prince and fairy godmother
both.

An Attempt for Anson

I tried
believe me I did
focused on his talent
pondered his supreme
propriety and incorruptibility
examined his sterling numbers
knew he tried to raise
game and players from infancy to
Pastime but
but

All I could see was the black error of
his dark-hearted convictions

Plus he couldn't field to
save his sorry ass

LUIS APARICIO (1934–)   *inducted in 1984*

How Heroes Are Made

Remembering the afternoon I bought
with my own money—fifteen cents— a lot
of pennies back when I was just a tot
of five or … sorry. I digress. I ought
to get back to my story. So I bought
a pack of baseball cards from Topps and not
those crappy cards that Fleer put out. They thought
that they could break that big Topps juggernaut
but soon they found … oops. Jeez, I overshot

my story. Where was I? Oh yeah, I bought
that pack of cards, my first. I'll tell you what —
I couldn't wait to see who all I got
and show them to my older brother Scott.
I ran to him and said "Hey look, I got...
the White Sox shortstop — Luis ... Apricot!"
With that, he started laughing and could not
stop telling all his buddies. I, distraught,
could not believe it, but I had begot
a brand new nickname, one I hadn't sought,
just 'cause I couldn't read so well. I thought
that Carrot-top or Pumpkin-head were not
so awful since my orange hair was what
was noticed. But this new one — APRICOT!
I hated him at first, but then we got
to watch him at Comiskey. Wow! He caught
a sinking liner in the hole then shot
a rope to first — a double play! And taught
the Yanks a stealing lesson they forgot:
If Looie's set to go, he won't get caught.
He even hit a triple, running hot
and, sliding headfirst, showed New York what's what!
Those other names the kids and I forgot.
They weren't, as nicknames go, worth diddly-squat.
They called me Looie right there on the spot.
Been with me as if tied on with a knot.
And now you've heard my story, so you're not
surprised to know I'm often overwrought
with pride. My orange-headed son can swat
line drives plus run and field: he's got a shot
to make it to the majors, but that's not
the reason that my eyes are so bloodshot:
he told me that he's lucky 'cause he's got
two heroes — me and Luis Apricot!

LUKE APPLING (1907–1991)   *inducted in 1964*

Good Wood

Crackerjack surprise
past Aches and Pains disappeared
new old slugging star

RICHIE ASHBURN (1927–1997)
AND MIKE SCHMIDT (1949–)   *both inducted in 1995*

All They Ever Wanted

All they ever wanted
    was to play it
    the way it was meant
    the way they were meant

The first, a White hot blur on the bases, in the outfield, leadoff incarnate
The other, no nickname, all business, refined essence of potent grace

All they ever wanted
    was to win
    for their team
    for their city
    for themselves

The first, a gee-Whiz early taste, but never next; his ring elusive as
    diamonds
The other disdained lettered titles or "me" trophies; failure's burn
    finally cooled in Series clutch

All they ever wanted
    when they knew
    was to leave
    on their own terms

The first, M. V. Met no honor, abdicated Polo throne; too soon for
   us, but for him, time
The other, a paragon frayed, limped away still, always, an All Star

> All they ever wanted
>> all they ever needed
>> was our love and respect

The first always knew his second home would always be here, yet
   doors of honor sealed tight
The other always certain of his perch in history, but not of his pur-
   chase in our hearts

And then, as our city limits stretched to Cooperstown in loving
   embrace

> They both got just what they wanted

> They both got just what they deserved

EARL AVERILL (1902–1983)   *inducted in 1975*

The Earl of Snohomish and Son

> He wasn't quite a junior but
> face it his name was yours
> doomed to a life of reflected
> failure though his talent was
> enough to carry him seven
> major league seasons they were lousy
> ones and though most fathers would
> beam and puff to say my
> son the ballplayer you could only
> shake your head and wonder where
> you went wrong

His Mom Called Him Frank

1922
riding the pine
end of the line
watching that big
baboon loft fast
rabbit balls into Yankee's
short right porch
you smiled secure
knowing that he
could park a
hundred but
never take
baseball's
ultimate
nickname

Dave Bancroft (1891–1972)   *inducted in 1971*

Beauty

How nice would it be
if we all had a friend
in the highest of places
who remembered the good
old days when we were
young and great and could
really do it and who
could get us in
teach us that
secret handshake
why it would be
a thing full of
Beauty

But very few of
us have our
very own
personal
Frankie
Frisch

Why This Bleacher Bum Hates Ernie Banks

How utterly simple for you
to constantly say let's play two.
While most of us fans have to work,
you stand there at first with a smirk
on your face. And why not? After all,
the Wrigleys pay *you* to play ball.
I wonder how long you would last
if somehow you got working-classed
and had to haul trash ev'ryday,
to smell bad for almost no pay.
Or sit at a desk and count beans
or stack and load tons of sardines.
You've got no idea how hard,
embittered, worn-out, battle-scarred
a life in the school of hard knocks
will make you. Instead all you jocks
get paid fifty times what we do.
It's all one more turn of the screw.
So
I'll drink beer and boo when I want
if
you so much as act nonchalant.
I paid my two bucks to get in,
I've earned it! I'll curse you, has-been!
Besides, my soul's Beelzebub's
already — I'm cursed for the Cubs!
I could've found pleasure in life
A respite from all of my strife.
My baseball team could've been winners:
I must be the worst of all sinners.
But the Cubs sure as hell ain't the Yanks.
No wonder I hate Ernie Banks!

Blue

If it is true that good
umps possess
uniquely
understated
inconspicuousness
then consider this
the ultimate compliment

ED BARROW (1868–1953)   *inducted in 1953*

Ed Barrow Would

routinely take credit
for having
astounding courage and
impeccable intelligence
in turning Ruth from
what he was to
what he was to
become

he felt
the same
post–BP
temptations
everyone else did
just
resisted
less

his genius
if any
wasn't for
man molding
or soul searching

The More Things

change	stay the same
ol' St. Jacob	just ninety-three hits to go
on another hot	just a few more at bats
spheroid	I'll be right back in the
smackin'	groove c'mon skip
spree	
screechin'	Love to play ya more
CHICKAZOOLA	ol' Jake but you are
to rattle them	forty now and .209
chowderhead	just won't cut it
chuckers	just can't carry you

Cool Papa in 1951

come play they said
but you'd had enough
got to settle down for
the family that city hall
night janitor gig looks
steady but cool the
majors nah the browns

although

cool papa in 1951
at forty-eight
was still better than
the best they had
except maybe
satch

Bench and My Brother

Oh man you saw it coming
from a mile away you saw it
coming you said
up three to two bottom nine Giusti on
just three outs and we're back in
the Series where we've been my
whole two year baseball life and
HEEEER'S JOHNNY
and my heart's humming like like
like maybe a zillion bees and the
big fat dodo-head waddles
to the plate helmet squashed down on his
big fat ugly head and he swings and misses
swings and hits one a zillion miles FOUL!
just one more Giust one more just
one BOOM climb the fence Roberto
CLIMB THE FENCE!!!
and my fifteen year old jerk brother
kept yelling I knew it I saw it coming the
whole time they're gonna lose for sure now
just wait and then they did and in my
devastated rage said between sobs
    Johnny Bench and you are
    are   are
    BASTARDS
my first cursing experience
successful and although I've since
forgiven my brother

CHIEF BENDER (1884–1954)   *inducted in 1953*

Just Charley

All they saw was red
They whooped the war cry while you
tried to pitch in peace

YOGI BERRA (1925–)   *inducted in 1972*

Although

You may not have said
all the things they said you said
your bat spoke volumes

JIM BOTTOMLEY (1900–1959)   *inducted in 1974*

Bottomley Whiten

Think about it
a dozen
twelve
That's a damned
career for most
Two Cards who really
cracked the nut for
at least one game
Ol' Sunny rode his day
all the way to the
Hall
But as for that Hittin' Mark
it's tough to squeeze
every ounce of
potential one day
and not expect it to
be expected the next

Boudreau at 31

at thirty-one
climbed as far and
high as can be
climbed
ss-mgr mvp play-off
WS CHAMPS

but

at thirty-one
couldn't quit though
he had to know
the pinprick
truth at the

core

so

at thirty-one

began the slide
unabated scraping
strawberry in totality
today boudreau blvd
fronts a parking garage

Himself

wanted
to be McGraw
who already was
so when he saw
Meyers squatting
at the wait and felt
the Duke of Tralee
starting down the trail
he gave his friend
the chance to be
him in St. Louis
but Roger found
he was sadly
no one but
himself

George Brett (1953–)   *inducted in 1999*

Sure but Kenny

was always the one
the high school stud who
got the girls got the press
got the bonus got the Series Call
while the little fat one stared and
dreamed to maybe be as good as

half a midwestern life later true
blue blood sovereignty from both
corners mixed with heroic red grit
the youngest still must dream as
the Father insists sure you were
good but Kenny could hit AND pitch

Lou's Limerick

There once was a thief name of Brock
Who felt second base was a lock
He picked it with ease
Then dusting his knees
Said "Save me the slide, and just balk."

DAN BROUTHERS (1858–1932)   *inducted in 1945*

Dan Brouthers at the Polo Grounds Press Gate

You'd think a man with
five batting titles and six
straight slugging crowns
might know a thing or two
but these kids they don't
wanna hear from Big Dan
they only see an old man
who stands at this damn door
but let me tell ya in my day I'da
kicked their asses so hard they'd
be sittin' on their heads and these
newspaper guys what a load a
crap they write not a one of em
ever played so how in hell can they
act like they's big experts I'll tell
ya this game is goin ta hell all they
think about is money what do you
think a man with five batting titles
oh, okay, you go on ahead in.
Like I was sayin you'd think a man

How Many Do You Want

if
you
knew
a few semi-
insignificant
digits in a corn
grinder for a few
short moments
would give you
a real shot as a
major league
pitcher
would
you
me
2

Morgan Bulkeley (1837–1922) *inducted in 1937*

Bull

you   election
me   before
anyone   this
who   politician
ever   figurehead
cared   league
about   president
baseball   who
deserves   clearly
          didn't

Kentucky Congressman's Election Wait Ends

Lefty
    ushered in by a landSLIDER
Schmitty
    elected after a great long distance campaign
Whitey
    waited patiently for leadoff platform to be recognized
And then the Congressman
    no longer four votes shy
    sidearm fastballs carried batter debates
    An American and multiNational Chief of Pitching Staffs
    perfect Father's Day dad gets his own perfect election day

Mr. Burkett After the 1921 Series

by Jesse Burkett (with assistance from the author)

You say I'm crabby but
I'm just misunderstood.
How can it be my fault
Your brains are made of wood.
To me your words assault
My dignity with smut.

To listen to you squawk
Offends my very core.
How dare you deign to speak!
Your thoughts induce a snore.
I wish you'd shut your beak,
And hear a genius talk.

I hit .400 thrice.
Alone that should convince
Your tiny minds that I'm
Superior. I wince
at swings committing crime.
But will you take advice?

Of course not! You're too dense
To realize you're blessed.
Despite your errors, my coaching
Has made this team the best.
My help, beyond reproaching:
Indeed, the difference.

So how could you deny
My rightful Series share?
Could you be more ungrateful?
I knew you all were ne'er-
Do-wells. You've been so hateful
To me, I wish you'd die.

You say I'm crabby but
I'm just misunderstood.

Campy Had

night dreams	**snap** throws
drive balls	**back** up
into corner	**first** base
slide safely	**dream** seasons
roll strikeout	**over** quickly
pitch back	**nightmares** soon
wreck Yankee	**began** mornings
cripple pitches	

The Maestro

Composer
stood composed
at home in the conductor's
box
a clear view of the orchestral
green
an ever so loose finger grip on
your baton
with mere flicks the
music began
woodwinds double
tongued down the
left line
pizzicato violin pluckings
over second and short
sharp trumpet line reports
directed to right
the startling crescendo of
fortissimo center percussive
blasts measured immediately
by pianissimo flutes
trilling lightly on the lines

each movement a perfect
harmony of art and action
you recorded 3053
symphonies

Stolen Base Carey

Maximilian Carnarius
the catcher thought him nefarious,
his situation precarious
when Scoops would reach first base.

He hoped mosquitoes malarious
Found him doubly nectarious.
The wishes for him multifarious
for ways he'd fall from grace.

Not shy, instead temerarious,
the felon was fond of gregarious
conversing. He found it hilarious
to taunt throughout the chase.

Despite behavior contrarious,
the backstop failed with his various
attempts to thwart omnifarious
thefts, and never saved face.

His final solution, viperious
was born of mood atrabilarious.
That desperate man, arbitrarious,
pegged down a can of mace!

No hope for the testudinarious,
turtle-like catcher's vagarious
idea, for ol' Max Carnarius
slid safe — with gas mask in place!

Cobra K for Carlton

perfect pitch pounce
Parker can't control his strike
mongoose slider slays

ALEXANDER CARTWRIGHT (1820–1892)   *inducted in 1938*

Alexander Cartwright Carried to Hawaii

A ball
THE ball
the FIRST ball
the Elysian Fields
        BALL

is it
just
dust

has it moldered into rich
peat sprouting round white and
red-striped flowers in the rainforest

does it bake stoically
a brilliant eyeball in
a frozen black sea of lava

do skeleton hands clutch
hugging to chalky chest
with paternal eternal love

does it surf the pipeline
skimming to a soggy stop
to catch some sandy rays

or

does it patiently rest in a
forgotten attic trunk like
Abner Graves' charlatan

waiting for another
chance to create
magic

ORLANDO CEPEDA (1937–) *inducted in 1999*

Baby Bull My Son

Looking
Confident in his own bronzed
Pedigree
Saw snap in pudgy wrists
Power in rounded frame
"He is my son," he declares
with jutty chin.
Future certain
Dreamed of them as teammates
one day

Looking
Pained by my own pitted
Genetics
Imagine snap in pencil wrists
Power in minuscule frame
"He is my son," I confess
with guilty shrug.
Future certain
Dream stubbornly of miracles
one day

Chadwick's Diamond

the
initial
reporter
rules maker
guide publisher
gambling opposer
his lasting gift
the boxscore
baseball's
original
poem

FRANK CHANCE (1877–1924)   *inducted in 1946*

Peerless Leader

they called him
back when
nicknames didn't
mess around and
though awkward
quaint and comical
today if you told him
that he'd most
likely shove a fist in
your mouth and ask if
you found anything
else about him
quaint

ALBERT CHANDLER (1898–1991)   *inducted in 1982*

Happy

dark walls
thick and tall as
Mountains
so easily
toppled by
logical
ethical
jocular
truth

OSCAR CHARLESTON (1896–1954)   *inducted in 1976*

The Best Player You Never Heard Of

looked like Ruth
batted   like Cobb
played   like Tris
colored like tar
the best player
you never heard of
still invisible
denied glorious
retrospection by
shadowy statistics

Not So Happy

454 and ⅔ innings
239 strikeouts
1.82 ERA
41 wins
and
all
they
can ever
think about
is 1 lousy wild
pitch on the last pitch
of the season and
though that year
landed me in
the hall
that
1
pitch
chased
me to my grave

Control Artist

For it to be all
It should
There must be limits
Blue painter's white line
dabbed into clay with chalk

Some

Granite power gargoyle glower
Confine with vise-like grip

Others

Brilliant chrome precision
chafe from prickly efficiency

Most

Crumble beneath cancerous frailty
Or widening flaw of variability

You

Economized elegance of
Space form and spirit and the
Euclidean perfection laser-ruled
immutability of your windowy clear
Strike zone

FRED CLARKE (1872–1960)   *inducted in 1945*

1909

eleven years
before there was
one
he played like Cobb
should be talkin bout
how he played like me
he said cept in
the series when I
kicked his rebel
ass back down south
cryin to his mama yeah
that Fall the Peach sure
was the pits

JOHN CLARKSON (1861–1909)   *inducted in 1963*

Finally

so I sit and
stare at the
engulfing
consuming
black hole screen
praying for it to
come but how
will he reach me
a century gone
star forgotten
beneath belmont
massachusetts
dirt for fifty-four years
until Cooperstown
finally ended his
long wait and mine

21 @ 65: '99

Island icon
Ruthian figure cut from Caribbean bronze
Tides of time leave white foamy crown
Like his father his face holds the look of eagles
Aged but not old
The Jíbaro ways still driving
Work
Share
Pride

He is not happy
To be happy is to be satisfied
He will never be

> They forget about me but
> for me I am the best
> No one throws better or
> Plays as hard
> But they forget
> Alou is old but they let him manage
> I know more than Alou forgets
> I manage in the Winter Leagues but they
> Will not give me a chance because
> I am black
> I am Latin
> I speak truth

No stateside statues
No Awards
No oldtimers games
No fantasy camps
No Social Security handouts
Only the Sports City

> I am still a man
> I can still work
> For me to work is all
> I am not ready yet to die

Road Rage

Heading home on the PA Turnpike
my eye catches in the rearview
a big old Caddy snapping through traffic
and I hear the roar as it grows so
I make my move around a sluggish
Exxon truck and I'm suddenly boxed
in by a rusty Dodge pickup then Caddy
zooms up and I feel the heat as
his windshield melts until I find a
hole and get shoved over as
he growls past so I check the plate
see the peach and below in smaller type
the county
and I'm almost surprised I don't feel
spike wounds on my back bumper

MICKEY COCHRANE (1903–1962)   *inducted in 1947*

Black Mike

just didn't get it
    first hint
the head weakens
mid season stress snaps
reality ability
        bigger hint
the head cracks
Bump Hadley beanball gives
last rights coma
but catcher heads are stubborn
he knew he'd rather die quick
a masked leader
then sit and watch in castrated
impotence
they said it was for his own
good but they
just didn't get it

Once

played second
batted second
pilfered second
with distinction
without a chin
but he missed his
true calling
his
one and only one
scouting trip
netted
Doerr and
T. Williams
there's two to stick
out your chin and
be cocky about
but why stop there
unless you quit for
once while on top

At Third Jimmy Collins First

Challenged
Hitters
A
Revolutionary
Genius
Extending
Defenses

Balletic
Ubiquity
Negated
Typical
Strategies

EARLE COMBS (1899–1976)   *inducted in 1970*

Convicted

quiet
as his silent e
a thief
stealthy profiteer
turning bunts to hits
singles to doubles to triples
unnoticed nickel and dimer
next to his homicidal teammates
after thirty-five years captured and
given life sentence of glory
of which he served just six years

CHARLES COMISKEY (1859–1931)   *inducted i*

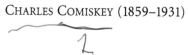

Commy

their dark deeds their own
mitigating fact remains
roman greed the root

JOCKO CONLON (1899–1989)   *inducted in 1974*

It's Not Like He Changed His Mind Either

although your bow tie wasn't hip
you figured out the way to win
your rhubarbs with Durocher's lip
you learned to stand in chin to chin
to counteract his gamesmanship
your method gave the umps a grin
with shinguards and a steel-toed tip
you forced the battle shin to skin

TOM CONNOLLY (1870–1961)   *inducted in 1953*

Sticker Shock

a ball
signed
would set
you back
a cool seven
grand today
a sum more
than any
one year's
salary

if he
were alive
it would
likely be
enough to
kill
the
umpire

ROGER CONNOR (1857–1931)   *inducted in 1976*

You Had One

last chance at fame
riding the babe as he
pounded his way
way beyond your
dusty dead ball drives
but
lanigan the figure filbert
fucked up the numbers
and no one knew you
were the guy and what good
does the hall of fame do
for a slugging skeleton

His Best Shot

a long time ago
at a bad party
with a big favor
blind date
for a forgotten friend
I met a girl
where are you from
I'm from Shamokin, PA
home of Stan Coveleski
hall of fame pitcher
you must love baseball
too no she said
they built a sign
oh I said and
then she walked away
thanks for trying Stan

Wahoo

a kid
reading about
hall of famers
biblical saints
in spikes and knickers
I saw his name
thought the fans
yelled it when
he came to bat
even though the story
explained about
Nebraska
thirty years later
I still prefer my version

a triple!

Wahoo!

JOE CRONIN (1906–1984)   *inducted in 1956*

Diehard

what the hell happened Joe
you were always a stand up
guy even sat down to let Pesky
play

so why were you the Red Sox's
Jim Crow never a dark face while
you were there
you couldn't kick them out of the
league but you damn well wouldn't honor
dying Jackie in 1972 no you just
sat that one out too

Bending the Truth

Fred Goldsmith made it official
in 1870 curving pitches around poles
but he didn't have Henry Chadwick
defense or the clean-up power of
the press on his side like Candy
who fired straight past the truth
into legend and Fame leaving
poor Fred forever spinning just outside
immortality under his own private
mound of frustration

KIKI CUYLER (1898–1950)   *inducted in 1968*

Mr. Cuyler

I never stuttered
not even muttered
my speech was plain as day
my nickname sprouted
when teammates shouted
for "Cuy" to make the play
and even though
as nicknames go
it might have left me surly
you'd quickly claim
another name
if yours was Hazen Shirley

Me and Ray Dandridge

five seven
one seventy
bowlegs
soft hands
nearly identical
neither of us could
play in the majors
except
I'm white without talent

Good Hiding Places

Lee Allen fueled
with scotch smokes
and a sacred quest
set up camp beside Cooperstown's
paper mountain and
began his excavation
mining for ballplayers
long buried pulling
nuggets of truth
diamond diamonds but
never the elusive
one George Davis
his Holy Grail
at search's end
with glorious discovery
a library built
an encyclopedia written
thank George

So Long Leon Day

so long
you waited
too long
they waited
they knew
we knew
you knew
but not
so long

LEON DAY (1910–1974)   *inducted in 1953*

Had Mark Twain Lived

to see him snicker and strut in
Sportsman's Park near enough to
to fire one clean into the big muddy
on the fly or so he'd boast

Had Mark Twain lived
to hear him pinch the hitters' egos
then stand behind his fastball as they
lined up for yet another whitewashing

Had Mark Twain lived
to wince from wicked irony as Averill's
All-Star liner caught him like Achilles
in the one unprotected place:
his patience

Had Mark Twain lived
surely Sam would have laughed to
find his sequel to *Tom Sawyer* already
penned in the flesh right there on the
hard-baked mound in Sportsman's Park

ED DELAHANTY (1867–1903)   *inducted in 1945*

Big Ed

your memory saved
Niagara fall refreshes
drowning you with Fame

BILL DICKEY (1907–1993)   *inducted in 1954*

Was It Rougher

watching him
on the set
repeat his
grandma throws
molasses
swings
or remembering
near the end
when the
real
man
wasn't
much
better

MARTÍN DIHIGO (1905–1971)   *inducted in 1977*

I Am

let Luque Marsans
other cubanos
pass
I am
Dihigo
I will play every
position in every
country and I will
laugh and sing and
everywhere I will triumph
and everywhere
they will remember
the Great Dark
Dihigo

JOE DIMAGGIO (1914–1999)   *inducted in 1955*

A Fisherman's Son

remember
a man can age
gracefully without
hiding his soul in a box
they call you a god
but must
you believe
you forget
no
cancers cured
battles won
children saved
you were
are
still
just
a fisherman's
son

Seconds

except at the
dinner table
America
could give a crap
about seconds
    second to play
        to manage
you were given a double
helping of discrimination
the first obvious but
you also weren't
Jackie

BOBBY DOERR (1918–)   *inducted in 1986*

In Every Picture of Bobby Doerr

you can plant corn
in his forehead
eyebrows pinched up
the middle forever
looking to turn two
eyes puzzling with
eternal haunting
   how is it
   we never
   won it all

DON DRYSDALE (1936–1993)   *inducted in 19*

Don Drysdale's Dinner Table

clean plate demanded
double order dirt-battered
ribs his specialty

HUGH DUFFY (1866–1954)   *inducted in 1945*

The Expert   Nice

Hugh who knew
  .438 in '94 on
  his résumé
  qualified

Fed Ted's head
  in '39 before
  .406 became
  his calling card

Concise precise advice
  Don't ever let 'em
  monkey with your
  form

For Leo on His Day

Back when it was baseball and
Hollywood and little else
You found yourself swept away
By the looks of him in suits.
Mexican divorce was a
Sin to Knothole moms but you
Couldn't wait a day longer
For Leo.

Half a century later
Impossible as that sounds
You found yourself swept away
Remembering him in suits.
Regular divorce so long
Ago seemed to close your show
As First Lady of Baseball
But you played that role once more
For Leo.

Billy Evans (1884–1956)   *inducted in 1973*

By the Book

young fastidious
teetotaling you
were something never
seen behind the plate
and for 22 years
you did it Sinatra-style
From the Inside

JOHNNY EVERS (1881–1947)   *inducted in*

Baseball's True Lexicon
(with Apologies to Franklin P. Adams)

These aren't the saddest of possible words,
    Tinker-to-Evers-to-Chance;
Trios aren't more than the sums of their thirds.
    Tinker-to-Evers-to-Chance?
Alley-to-Maz-to-Clendenon's the way
this poem should read, not some ancient cliché,
and what the heck's gonfalon mean anyway?
    Tinker-to-Evers? NO CHANCE!

BUCK EWING (1859–1906)   *inducted in 1939*

Buck Ewing on the Cover of
an 1889 Harper's Weekly

I must ask   Your
Dunno Got some old   dim
ones Look over there   paper filtered
                              voice

Here I am
I think I hear   lies to me
muffled beneath
musty dusty   again
daunting stacks

A thousand times
sifted for you
stiff back
dirty hands
wasted afternoons

Red's Blues

had red's arm
been in the pink
those yellow backed
green sniffers
couldn't have
hatched their
black scheme
since lily white red
woulda whitewashed reds

BOB FELLER (1918–)   *inducted in 1962*

Poor Judgment

fifteen years before
you declared your '62
classmate
Class D at best
won't hit you were sure
too muscled in the chest
he's not much of a player
only for his color
no wonder you ain't
a scout

RICK FERRELL (1905–1995)   *inducted in 1984*

No More No Wes

The Hall of Fame gave him the nod
in 1984.
The writers felt the choice was flawed,
but here's a heretofore
unchecked and unsubstantiated
rumor as to why
a candidate so weak was rated
obviously high.
The Vets Committee got mixed up
(it happens when you're old).
They had to plan a cover-up
to keep the tale untold.
A vow of silence never works,
the truth so hard to smother.
The records make it plain: Those jerks!
They meant the other brother!

ROLLIE FINGERS (1946–)   *inducted in 1992*

Save

you came in when
a save was a save
and killed instead
you twirled your Dick
Dastardly curls
tied the rally
to the tracks
and let the A-train
run her over

Savior

How did it feel they gush
to be the oracle
to be the miracle
to be the answer to
the fervency of millions
to be the native son redeemer
to be for one
      pitch
      swing
      tightrope dance
      skip
      leap home
Jesus Christ himself
in the home whites

He shrugs and with a
Vermonter's priority
replies
we lost

ELMER FLICK (1876–1971) *inducted in 1963*

Only Elmer

Who is this Flick
He ain't the Mick
His stats no overwhelmer
The only claim
To prove his Fame
He'll be the only Elmer

Our Eddie Whitey Ford

there was an ed ford
in my neighborhood
eddie we called him
except the summer
when he made the Hall
whitey he became
his hair was straw blond
but it didn't stick
we all liked the mets
whenever my dad
saw him he would say
Mr. chairman then
asked if he was "board"
laugh and walk away
took me nineteen years
before I got it

willie the painter

bill foster
who?
Rube's half-brother
as fine a lefty there was that
nobody ever heard of
nobody white anyway
in twenty-nine gehringer said
    if I could
    paint you white
    I could get
    100,000 for
    you right now
but the only painting to be
done
was on the black

RUBE FOSTER (1879–1930)   *inducted in 1981*

Rube

start with
Mathewson
add equal parts
McGraw
and Ban Johnson
mix until dark

dead at 51
he lived
153 years

The Good Fight

The clichés allied against you like the Maginot Line

TOOSMALLZEROPOWERNOPROSPECT

But you had some ammunition of your own
        GOODGLOVE
        CAN'TTEACHSPEED
        PLAYSEVERYDAY

And in the end

            staccato sniper attacks
                with choked bat
            head-first forays against armed
                catcher cannons
            steady Red Man–stained defense

Earned you your posthumous laurels

But for nineteen years it was
                    PLAY
            Putting the ball in
            Making the routine
            Forcing them to make the

That won you your proudest reward

        A majors uniform

Most Walxx in a Game—Sixx

The Browns against the Soxx
Afraid of Jimmie's knoxx
no pitches came
close to his frame
when in the batter's boxx

through these unorthodoxx
attempts at stopping Foxx
they lost the game
despite their aim
a run/walk paradoxx

FORD FRICK (1894–1978)   *inducted in 1970*

Frick's Fault

grimly gripped
drinking days
past particular
schoolgirl swoon
Bambino barrister
rejected reality
rearranged records
absurd asterisk
murdered Maris

Hurry Up

that's what McGraw
taught
be quick
be ready
be first
skipped
the minors
slipped into
starting lineup
zipped to
player-manager
later couldn't stand
watching lazy fat
modern players waste
time
clipped a guardrail at
75 doing 95 on I 95
still listening
to his manager

Pud's Retort

Controversial pick
was dead for sixty-three.
The writers wrote,
"They shouldn't vote
a mere footnote.
It gets our goat,
such vast stupidity."

Galvin's rhetoric
came down from overhead:
"Such animus
is onerous.
It's obvious
I'm worthy, plus
it's not my fault I'm dead!"

LOU GEHRIG (1903–1941)   *inducted in 1939*

1938

a vintage Mustang
still powerful classic but
rusting from within

CHARLIE GEHRINGER (1903–1993)   *inducted in 1949*

Wind Him Up

so I asked him what
he'd want me to write about

No poems for me.
All I did was do my job,
not talk about it.

too late thanks Charlie

BOB GIBSON (1935–)   *inducted in 1981*

Gibbie's Tune

never got it with the Trotters
Aretha Franklin had it right
demanded received your propers
batters flailed away at high heat
released just inches from the plate
relieved to escape from danger
ancient self-preserving instincts
shared in the safe shade of dugouts
until the inevitable end when rookies
unexposed to your dominance
found your fury less threatening
than veteran memories held and
when Pete LaCock swung — from the heels!
ripping slam humiliation
no longer was it yours to command

Josh

did not die
of a broken
heart
because it was
Jackie and not him
although it was
when he did

Warren Giles (1896–1979)   *inducted in 1979*

Shut Up Warren

when it was Marvin Miller
v. Lords of Baseball and
minimum salary was up a
whopping grand in twenty years
one Lord who said oh my
that's awful didn't sit in on
negotiations after that

Lords have mercy the
truth shall get you free

time

Lefty

clean living fast outfield
but Triple Crowns don't
happen by chance
while lucky to be a Yankee
on the mound you were no
joke

GOOSE GOSLIN (1900–1971)   *inducted in 1968*

Goose on Trial

There once was a Tiger called Goose
who wished for an Indian truce.
With his fourth double play,
still a record today,
the Tribe laughed, "Him cry like papoose."

His teammates would hear no excuse.
Support for their case was profuse.
They said, "Take a gander!"
He replied, "This is slander!"
Their lawyers charged Goose with abuse.

"He's guilty," the judge did deduce,
"and by law we must cook Goose's goose."
His feathers got ruffled,
but his protest was muffled,
and they hung Goslin's bat with a noose.

Not Jackie but Still

his people's hero
wished to be remembered as
player not symbol

Clark Griffith (1869–1955)   *inducted in 1946*

Clark Griffith Took His

coffee with cream
but he couldn't take
them black
smoked out Cubans long
before Castro
but only if they
were mild
back home
their rent was green enough
their talent strong enough
but his palate was never
bold enough for anything but
coffee with lots and lots of
cream

BURLEIGH GRIMES (1893–1985)   *inducted in 1964*

Ol' Stubblebeard

There was no bigger sourpuss
than bad old Burleigh Grimes
and no he wasn't interviewed
for *Glory of Their Times.*
He didn't make the Hall for how
he pitched with spit. Instead
he threatened, "Vote for me or
I'll chuck fastballs at your head!"

He'da been on your ballot, too.

LEFTY GROVE (1900–1975)   *inducted in 1947*

Lefty's Arm

was
an arrogant prick
hated anything that breathed
refused
to accept any
failure hurling
blame like
brushbacks it
took Fenway and
a tank finally emptied of
all the fast and furious to
turn regular
it learned doing it all
alone
wouldn't feed the chickens
anymore

◆ 59 ◆

K HAFEY (1903–1973)   *inducted in 1971*

Iffy Chicky Hafey

no offense chick but
what the hell are you doing
in my book all I hear is if
if his sinuses and
if his eyes and
if I only had
size strength quickness
balls talent right now I'd
be writing a damn poem about
myself

JESSE HAINES (1893–1978)   *inducted in 1970*

Jesse Haines Knocked Down

the Berlin wall
yes he did
I know he was a
decade dead but
if he doesn't get
that bleeding
blister then ol' Alex doesn't
come in drunk and punch
out Poosh 'em up and
Reagan isn't in that movie
cause there ain't one and
so he don't get
elected and them pinko
commie homersexules
would still be there
damn right I'm right

◆ 60 ◆

SLIDING BILLY HAMILTON (1866–1940)   *inducted in 1961*

Safe

fossil archetype
role unearthed from headfirst dust
the leadoff leadoff

NED HANLON (1857–1937)   *inducted in 1996*

Just Win Baby

his philosophy
long before Lombardi
Vince not Ernie
he invented how
to win
the right way
and looked away
when his O's also learned
the wrong way
maybe he was more
Davis
Al not George

An Ode to Will Harridge
by Eddie Gaedel
as related by the author

Examining your record proves me right
You're worthless, just a baseball parasite.
Any little change from status quo
was voted down, dismissed, malapropos.
Of course night baseball went against your grain:
so obvious ... for people with a brain!
You took the credit for the All-Star Game
despite the fact the Negroes had the same.
But all those other faults are nothing next
to what you did to me without pretext.
I had a legal contract! That's a fact!
We should have known you'd just overreact.
But how could you remove my single stat,
you jealous, pompous, midget-hating rat!
You always were a frumpy gloom and doomer.
It's clear you never had a sense of humor.
You'll see: there'll be a special place in hell
for wiping out the walk of Ed Gaedel!

Boy

they saw you win the
double switch battle with
McGraw (!) at twenty-seven for the
Senators (!) in '24 and never
forgot your genius and
twenty-two hundred losses (!)
later they were still letting you
prove it was
by the time you were a man
all used up

Nicknames

Charles Leo was never much for
words so of course they called him

So today I guess we ought
to call them

Poor

Posthumous

17 summers	17 summers
in the bigs	in the booth
uphill climb	uphill climb
in Detroit	in Detroit
to slugger	to Ol' Slug
arthritis	beloved voice
gone too soon	gone too soon

to Cooperstown
too late

BILLY HERMAN (1909–1992)   *inducted in 1975*

Billy Herman's Buddy, Mired

	1922	1923
Games Played		
Batting Average	.304	.303
Slugging Pct.	.407	.406
Runs	1163	1174
RBI	839	850

There's more but you've gotten the gist.
If you can distinguish between them,
you must have seen something I missed.
Identical fruit from the same stem:
No sweat for a good botanist.
But no one can offer a theorem
why Bill's in but Bud's off the list.

HARRY HOOPER (1887–1974)   *inducted in 1971*

Postmaster—Capitola, Calif.

Neither rain
nor cleat
nor looming fights
could sway this
right field harrier
from his anointed crown.

ROGERS HORNSBY (1896–1963)   *inducted in 1942*

Rogers' Life

while you watched the rest
slog through our
handle sting weak
twelve hopper to short
lives
never sure whether to
tag up or sprint for home
or even who or what was
calling us out or
safe
you refused to believe yours
could be anything but a
round on round square shot
line drive up the gap or
unworthy
of consideration its entirety
defined only by your vain
view from inside
corner to outside black
edge

WAITE HOYT (1899–1984)   *inducted in 1969*

Past Tense

found mound
success with
hometown pinstripes
and forevermore
looked back
while the past fattened
and bloated even as
he broadcast dingy red
games a few tense moments
behind

CAL HUBBARD (1900–1977)   *inducted in 1976*

Lineman

crouching
dreaming
hoping they'd
give him just
one chance
        brawl
        caterwaul
        over a call
to show why
their Giant fear
was founded
their rushing respect
required

King Carl's Arm

Cobb was right
hell the damn pitch
screwed it clear around
so you had to clap
like a seal but
you just let the fans
do yours for you

CARL HUGGINS (1879–1929)   *inducted in 1964*

Ruth Kills Huggins

the ceaseless battle
for the right to be there
a small man in the bigs
then the neighborhood
bully looms once again
and the battle flares anew
one step back
one day's rest
is suicide

finally
when the war front
was only within
you found your
cache exhausted
arms depleted
you surrendered with
little resistance while
the bully wept his bitter
confession

WILLIAM HULBERT (1832–1882)   *inducted in 1995*

A Century Later, the Union

first to find the clause
took it all from the players
reserved for owners

JIM HUNTER (1946–1999)   *inducted in 1987*

The Three Million Dollar Man

you'd think a good ol' boy
from the sticks of North Caroline
woulda took that fifty grand from
ol' Charlie O late or not shoved it
in his vest pocket and walked away
whistlin' Dixie but ol' Jim was
sharper 'nat and by the time them
big city owners were done trippin'
all over theyselves ol' Jim was
halfway to Lee Majors

MONTE IRVIN (1919–)   *inducted in 1973*

Standards

we all thought
it had to be you
you had it all
body and soul
when you first heard
about Jackie
it was everything
and nothing at all

It Wasn't Reggie

'86 playoffs and
we're watching
my roommate and
I and here's a big
spot and up he comes
it's October after all
my roommate from
boston remembers '78
says christ not him again
but it is
so dangerous
so much clutch behind
every twisting uppercut

but

no towering blast or rope
to right not even a
breathtaking whiff just a
routine five hopper to second that
ends the inning
relieved my roommate laughs he
sucks and the shot of reggie's
shocked face agrees
it wasn't him after all

Next

quietly
slipped on
Bancroft's
giant spikes
and
for fifteen
years shined
his own way
a polished
path to
immortality

---

pick 'em out

robin jenkins hunter ferguson catfish roberts
fastball slider challenge strikeouts homeruns
catfish ferguson robin hunter roberts jenkins
twentywin seasons completegames no walks
ferguson roberts catfish jenkins hunter robin
twohundredplus wins lotsofinnings staffaces
jenkins ferguson roberts robin hunter catfish
righthanders power pitchers cooperstowners
ferguson jenkins robin roberts catfish hunter

Attorney Out Law

Before it even started
the bailiff felt a whack.
He never saw it coming
from behind.
Stenographer departed,
her fingers blue and black,
the rookie lawyer simply
disinclined
to have his discourse charted.
The judge's cardiac
resulted when the lawyer screamed,
"You're blind!"
The jury soon imparted,
"Kind sir, do not attack!
"A guilty verdict's soon to be
assigned!"
Defense was chicken-hearted:
Who was this maniac?
His actions were so grossly
unrefined.
It should've been expected
he'd test the rules for slack,
when Eeh-Yah practiced law and
ball combined.

Czar

didn't recognize the fall
when it came
seven years before
a wild snowy peak
casting inexorable shadow
over his kingdom

Judy Judy

Robert Edward Gans
would be little more than
the faintest of black blips
in the statistical universe
no more known than any
other decent but definitely
not great negro outfielder
from the teens and twenties
except that by miracle of
genetic differentiation
recombinant dna
happenstance
ie luck
William Julius Johnson
looked so much like him
don't know when he was
born or died but we know
his stats and his nickname
which after all ain't nothin

WALTER JOHNSON (1887–1946)   *inducted in 1936*

Johnson, Walter 4/16/98

(handwritten: 187?)

decent size but thin and gangly
might fill in
good speed but no other pitches
sidearm motion, poor mechanics
arm won't last long without changes
does not field position well
can hit but won't need with DH
question his will to win
is afraid to come inside
too easygoing

can't recommend as a ML prospect

(handwritten: Scouting report ?)

ADDIE JOSS (1880–1911)   *inducted in 1978*

Addie and Applegate

the bargain so simple too simple
make me utterly invincible today
            and you were
but you didn't take many business
classes in college and besides he
wrote the book on the art of the deal
            half game out
with every pitch that day your arm
            grew ever older
as did your soul and impatient for
instant gratification as always he took you
            down soon after

Black and White

born four months and one day
apart
they played right right yet
as different as
hot latin jazz riffs against
methodical timepiece perfection
starburst against sunrise and
sunset
spicy pumpernickel lashing
against solid white bread stroke
yet Pirate from the caribbean
and blue collar assembly line
Tiger ended just seven
hits separated equally
beloved

TIM KEEFE (1857–1933)   *inducted in 1964*

Like the Bugs Bunny Cartoon

There once was a pitcher named Keefe
who brought many batters to grief.
With his change he'd entice,
on one pitch they'd swing thrice,
so his slow pitch still kept the games brief.

WILLIE KEELER (1872–1923)   *inducted in 193*

Wee

death by mosquito
bat and feet malarial
thousand single bites

GEORGE KELL (1922–)   *inducted in 1983*

How the Kell Is He In?

in '92 I listened to them
introduce him as a
hall of famer

HALL OF FAMER

how could I not know a
hall of famer I who could
name every 500 homer
guy plus his total every
3000 hit 300 win every

I looked him up
and found out

JOE KELLEY (1871–1943)   *inducted in 1971*

Life and Death

moment remembered
resurrected briefly soared
dust he did return

GEORGE KELLY (1895–1984)   *inducted in 1973*

Pocket Watch

April 1921
seven homers
papers printed
Ruth Watch
first time
May 1921
watch stopped
September 1921
twenty-three total
time's up

MIKE "KING" KELLY (1857–1894)   *inducted in 1945*

The Soul of a King

given its unconditional
release in november
left boston flew down
the coast until its option
was picked up in Baltimore
three months later above
Big George Sr.'s place a
saloon of course

HARMON KILLEBREW (1936–)   *inducted in 1984*

Harm

resembled his name
not in the bar but the
proof of 0.20 seconds
pure distilled violence
in the box

RALPH KINER (1922–)   *inducted in 1975*

Kiner's Korner

everyone knows you as the light bulb
nosed clown prince of the gaffe but
there was a time when you were it
on a stick with the big stick the long ball
king stud Liz Taylor Janet Leigh riding
shotgun in that big caddy pulling down the
large green but today
when you glance in the
rear view which guy looks back

CHUCK KLEIN(1904–1958)   *inducted in 1980*

Any Number of Chuck Klein's

had that rusty right Baker Bowl
fence scraping his back to thank
for some even most but geez not
all and try as they might to keep him
out there was in the end just too much

BILL KLEM (1874–1951)   *inducted in 1953*

Catfish

drew chasms
canyons
vast fissures
in the dirt
with his authority
unbreachable
openings
connected
directly
to the
showers

SANDY KOUFAX (1935–)   *inducted in 1972*

Remember That

Hell yeah it was me that faced him
lost the damn game on a lousy
        damn ball four call and lousy
        damn throw I was just as in command
as him but he gets the perfect game and
all the luck and all the money but Don Hendley
who the hell is he even though five days later I
beat the s.o.b. 2–1 with a four hitter
too but does anybody else   hell no
so shut up and pour me another one dammit

NAPOLEON LAJOIE (1874–1959)   *inducted in 1937*

Nap

found joy in the battle
savage grace elegant
defense powerful clubbings
his war without arrogance
subtly conquering hero who
embraced foes without
exile

KENESAW LANDIS (1866–1944)   *inducted in 1944*

Mountain

a judge's dream job
power of God no appeals
great world series seats

TOM LASORDA (1927–)   *inducted in 1997*

Blue Blood

How is it that a
          stocky Italian kid from the meanest
          streets of Norristown PA hard
          on the edge of the South Philly
          Mafia with a big mouth bassett hound
          eyes and a bp curve finds himself in
Brooklyn NY
          for two very lukewarm cups of
          coffee then to KC MO proving himself
          a bonafide minor league non-prospect
          then fifteen years of bus rides bad
          pasta and beers all the way to
Los Angeles CA
          where Series followed Series and
          Hollywood came to schmooze while the
          lasagna and cannoli came as fast
          as the hugs and one-liners and
          after twenty-five years ends up in
Cooperstown NY
          hugging a bronze plaque letting tears
          of pride flow like a nice Merlot
          trying to explain
          how it is
          that
          a

TONY LAZZERI (1903–1946)   *inducted in 1991*

Poosh 'Em Up

it's there   never on
in the eyes   the field in 14
the strain of a   seasons but how
life lived   in fear   could he   be sure
of the known   carpe diem his
unknown   malocchio

BOB LEMON (1920–2000)   *inducted in 1976*

Lem

reverse Ruth
you got the job
he always wanted
but to be The Boss'
antidote for Billy
would leave anyone
sour

BUCK LEONARD (1907–1997)   *inducted in 1972*

1950

Gray from way back
when you all were
separate together
Gray home steady
power and flash
last busride back
tires on cobblestone
the last gray rumble
of the last of the
thunder twins

FRED LINDSTROM (1905–1981)   *inducted in 1976*

Freddie Lindstrom and the HOF Conspiracy
by Oliver Stone (as recorded by the author)

don't you see it
the 1924 Series
the Senators
Walter Johnson's last chance
the administration NEEDED a win
the pebbles
the "hits"
the immediate absolution
then later COOPERSTOWN
look at the record
they bought his silence
you must understand
Johnson could NOT be permitted
to escape the Series
a loser

The Ties That Bind

Leonard, Buck   yeah, ok
Lindstrom, Fred   the pebble guy
Lloyd, John   who?

       Chrissy's British ex?
       wait, who is he I know
       everybody I HAVE to
       how could there be
       a HOFer … oh
       okay just POPped into
       my head

Lost

out of the game for fourteen
years lost each
day brought closer
to willard's face
lost in his vacuumous eyes
his wry smile saying

not long now Dad
And i won't leave the mess you did
You left You everywhere
pooling on tile dripping down walls flowing through me
left the son to improve on the Father's legacy
i'll make you proud Dad it'll be so clean
just an on-deck kneel above the tub
one last cut
no runs no hits no heirs none left

Ernie asked his eyes how

how could he

they answered how

how could i not

Ernie walked into the bathroom
locked it behind him

The Weekend

I gotta quit going up there he
says every year be almost ninety
getting so I don't fit in anyway
buncha damn millionaires now
that s.o.b. reggie jackson calling
me gramps hell didn't even play
against more'n a few that're left
that come anyway but I still managed
against quite a few and handed ol'
reggie a few splinters up his ass
with slow curves away and smiling
picks up the phone dials his travel agent

Prophet

you had it licked for crissakes
working just one day a week
south side congregations flocked
worshipped each summer Sabbath
your own sermon on the mound
then you had to sip the cup
become sacrificial skip
despite every fervent prayer
could not convert apostles'
Judas gloves and bats and arms
your Sox had no Lazarus
resurrection miracle

NNIE MACK (1862–1956) *inducted in 1937*

#1

Records come and records go,
but mine won't get the old heave-ho
till Lucifer's an Eskimo.

Ask the Babe, he's got few left.
And Cobb's are holding by a weft.
Why even Gehrig's now bereft.

Skippers know: the towel's been tossed.
Most Games is mine, both Won and Lost.
Today they're never boss, just bossed.

LARRY MACPHAIL (1890–1975) *inducted in 1978*

Boom

reveled in the possibilities
the journey the thing not
the destination
the center of the swirling
storm master architect
but never maintenance man
he always saved the last stick
of dynamite for himself

LEE MACPHAIL (1917–)   *inducted in 1998*

Not His Father's Son

the man who says nothing
not exactly a prerequisite
for Cooperstown but maybe
they were all just so thankful
this chip wasn't from his dad's
shoulder

MICKEY MANTLE (1931–1995)   *inducted in 1974*

The Mick

I'm sick of the mick
and this tragedy crap
face it anyone of us
even if we knew we'd live to
a hundred would trade lives in a
new york yankee minute
and wouldn't do a
damn thing different either
except maybe that theresa
brewer
song

First Stooge Ejected from WS Game

Spleeny meanie Heinie, Moe
Howard-esque, he grabbed his bow
tie, and said "You so and so!
"Change your call, or I'll let go…"
Then Heinie got the old heave-ho.

RABBIT MARANVILLE (1891–1954) *inducted in 1954*

Back from the Minors

There once was a shortstop named Rabbit
whose drinking was too strong a habit.
In earnest he said,
"Once high-spirited.
"Now, Prohibited
"I have but one dread —"
"If I lose my sobriety, grab it!"

JUAN MARICHAL (1937–)   *inducted in 1983*

Deliveries

curve slider screw and fast
under side three quarters over the
top
high kick or slide step
only one he didn't have
was one they could hit
could also be dangerous
on occasion with
the bat

RUBE MARQUARD (1889–1980)   *inducted in 1971*

True Glory

the worst of the best
praise with faint damning
thanked Mr. Ritter everyday
for the boost
although his times were as
glorious as they come
the power of the pen
is sometimes mightier than
the numbers

Eddie Mathews Waits

at the table surrounded
by show toadies looking so
very tired

    how has it come to this
    hit 512 and still it wasn't
    enough
    never enough

waits
none in his line
for hours

waits
to get to the
hotel bar

waits
until he's finally not an
ex-ballplayer
anymore

CHRISTY MATHEWSON (1880–1925)   *inducted in 1936*

Pictures of Matty

always more beautiful in
uniform than out as if
there was where he
was created to
forever and
only be
for us
all

WILLIE MAYS (1931–)   *inducted in 1979*

Say Hey

God's own ballplayer
an abandoned sculpture
who you are
eroded
to past tense
when they gush at you of
what you were
you see the snarling
what am I now

Ralph Garr, Realistic

takes an optimistic hack at a 3–1 Blass cut fastball
rolls one to second jogs two steps down the line
then veers off toward the bench and up in the
booth Prince goes absolutely off his rocker

whatshedoinganythingcanhappen
youneverknowtheyvegottafineor
benchhimidontcarehowgoodheis
hecouldstilldroponeeveryonedoes
eventhebestheckIveseenitandwhile
hecanstillpickithesnotwhatheonce
wasbutthenagainwhotheheckisand

Ralph knowing full well the storm that would soon
follow still cannot help but see in that oh so routine
grounder with the high school handle hop the utter
hopelessness of man's quest for immortality the bane
of our earthly existence the inevitability of our eventual
destruction and simply chooses to exercise control over
the one variable left to him the timing of his own end and
as he heads straight to the showers mutters over and over

death taxes rollers to Maz

Marse Joe

was never alone even
when locked in the bathroom
    sweating out every detail of
    his next enemy even
when he felt Hornsby horn in even
when MacPhail bounced him even
when he picked Galehouse even
when picked up out of a Detroit gutter

he had his job
he had his flask

when he finally lost the one
he found he didn't even need
the other

TOMMY MCCARTHY (1863–1922)   *inducted in 1946*

Heavenly × 2

luck of the irish
beside duffy forever
beantown paradise

Stretch Fire Wince Duck

my job was to create it
in them not the other
way around felt
I was quick enough
cat like they said
wouldn't happen to me
it never entered my mind
until
McCovey

JOE McGINNITY (1871–1929)   *inducted in 1946*

Iron Clad Facts

pitching doubleheaders isn't much
spend a month in a foundry you'll
find out what real work is besides
the day I stop throwing's the day I
start dying

BILL McGOWAN (1896–1954)   *inducted in 1992*

Iron Man

more than Gehrig
more than Ripken
over 16 years
2541 games
22869 innings man
that's a helluva lotta
boos pinging off your
fire-forged confidence

JOHN McGRAW (1873–1934)   *inducted in 1937*

Muggsy in '32

taunting red cape
he still took the bait
every time
his demands for respect
muted by the cartoon
shadow of squatty mediocrity

BILL McKECHNIE (1886–1965)   *inducted in 1962*

Deacon

through both good and bad
percentages his savior
faithful to "the book"

McPhee(s)

I think that we shall never see
A player manly as McPhee
McPhee whose calloused hands so tough
Could snag a dart without a muff
McPhee who pilfered hitters' hits
By robbing them with mittless mitts
Indeed McPhee was quite beloved
For he was last to play ungloved
A man with skin of such renown
No doubt belongs in Cooperstown
Gloves are made for wimps like me
But not for real men like McPhee

JOE MEDWICK (1911–1975)   *inducted in 1968*

Ducky-Wucky

a career red-ass
but even mister tough guys
get humbled by the
inevitable fastball
to the temple
after that
he really resembled
that asinine nickname
both toes and then the
head too

Johnny's DeMize

I'm really not so sure that it is wise
to make this poem's verses rhyme with Mize.
Perhaps if I explain you'll sympathize,
if not I, in advance, apologize.
At first I thought I'd simply eulogize,
but didn't think it right to moralize.
Instead another plan began to rise.
His feline nickname! I could "lionize"
or try to backward anthropomorphize!
The muses called, but all I heard were cries
of "Cliché! Cliché!" I had no replies.
So moving on I looked to analyze
his record. Maybe it personifies
the man. I stared and searched until my eyes
were tired and blood-shot: no such stat applies.
I even thought I'd joke about his thighs
and how they sometimes grew to oversize.
He might be easy for some other guys.
But in the end I have no alibis.
You know the type, so easy to despise.
They'd churn one out within a couple tries.
So now I hope you've come to realize
I had no other choice to exercise.
I called Kevorkian to euthanize
this poem.

Little Joe

didn't seem great to me
growing up
just hated his chicken-wing
flapping always on base way
in the hole toy glove
beating my bucs
didn't seem great
but kids all over the country
just hated his chicken-wing
flapping

STAN MUSIAL (1920–)   *inducted in 1969*

A Bad Hunk of Metal

Stan
deserved to have a statue cast in bronze
The Man
greatest of the baseball Card icons
Can
you imagine feeling more unusual
than
gazing at your likeness so unMusial!

Prince Hal

it was my heart they said
my heart
what could I do if they wouldn't
take me
Pee Wee and Joe D and hell
most guys
played ball the whole damn war I
played too
just in the majors and when they
came back
I still got 'em out so you won't hear
me apologize
for a single damn thing 'cause I know
I belong

KID NICHOLS (1869–1953)   *inducted in 1949*

With

no wind
no curve
no change
just speed
to spots
and nerve
with ball
in hand
kid was
all man

Kniekro

If there ever was a kname
That should start with a "k"
Both for what you threw and
The inevitable consequences

> knoisily
> knauseating
> knear-misses
> knecessitating
> knightmarish
> knose diving
> knumbers
> knullified
> knattering
> knaysayers

While we're changing it
Your full kname
Ought to have been

 <u>W</u>illiam <u>P</u>hilip

Initially

At least according to
your catchers who couldn't

Words

started it all with
a sharp liner to
left
letting his bat talk
for a change
120 years and millions
of base knocks later
it's my turn at
the plate
looking for a word
I can drive
the opposite way

MEL OTT (1909–1958)   *inducted in 1951*

Nice Guy

he tried
he really did
he'd fine and hang us
in the press himself got
doubleheader doublethumbed
even lippy never did that he said
but we all saw through
the charade of tough
his powerful acute
benignancy
terminal but
he tried

Satch

while
there was
a
black
gehrig
black
ruth
black
cobb
black
matty
nobody
will
ever
be
a
white
you

Not Even

even O's fans
shared guilty
delight
watching his
comeback crash
in an ash cacophony
not
even Mr. Perfects
should get to
win the lottery
more than once

Ever Hear of Camp Skinner,
Norm McMillan, and George Murray?

yet another yank
yanked from evil clutches of
envious left wall

1975

Seventh and final round his team
still staggering from Fisk's
roundhouse right couldn't solve
Spaceman's bob and weave
his red-faced whiff in round two
remembered the hippie
telegraphed the same slop curve

    spinning sleepily in the
    New England night
    he could see reflected
    with crystal clarity all
    the hard steamy days before
    Fidel the long self-doubting
    Sally rides framed by tobacco
    leaves and he saw his father
    now and always a reluctant
    Red still smoothly stroking
    clean lines through pithy sweet
    stalks so he waited and waited

and with that same powerful swing
sent his sleepy Reds a wake-up smack
deep into the New England night that
knocked out Lee and took the decision

Gaylord

Perhaps he didn't have the greatest
fastball in the league.
His curveball didn't break real sharp, his
change held no intrigue.
The reason why he holds a Cy Young
trophy in both hands
is Gaylord Perry's Hall of Famer
salivary glands.

GETTYSBURG EDDIE PLANK (1875–1926)   *inducted in 1946*

College Man

an early Freudian perhaps
dissecting batters' ego dreams
much more likely Pavlovian
making them slobber for a strike
or even pre–Skinner the box
ideal lab for feeble brains
though he didn't actually
take classes at Gettysburg C.
he still was *magna cum laude*
with a doctorate in crafty southpaw

Dear Puck,

I write, I must confess,
beneath a mountain of duress.
To naked truth I'll acquiesce:
You ARE a Hall of Famer.

My buddies at the local bar
were sure you'd make it in by far.
First ballot for a superstar,
a true blue Hall of Famer.

But I was not so free from doubt.
I thought, "What's all this crap
        about?
"Did Kirby *really* make you shout,
'There goes a Hall of Famer'?"

The reason I was cynical:
Your shape was so … cylindrical!
To me you looked too comical,
not like a Hall of Famer.

The loyalty my friends attach?
They proudly give their guts a
        scratch
insisting their physiques can
        match
at least ONE Hall of Famer's.

Of course I now indeed admit
your pedigree is exquisite,
fulfilling each prerequisite
to be a Hall of Famer.

I trust your kindly reputation
permits, with little trepidation,
my short request: a small donation,
you HUMAN Hall of Famer.

'Cause here's the deal. I lost the bet
with ev'ryone, so I'm in debt
for drinks and lunch: my great
        regret
that you're a Hall of Famer.

I hope you'll be a true adult
and dip into your endless vault.
'Cause after all, it's not MY fault
that you're a Hall of Famer!

You're tops in Hall of Famerhood!
I need it soon, so if you would
a check, or cash, or M.O.'s good.

                Sincerely,
                    Pass N. Blamer

Providence

sat alone deep in darkened corner
hiding his shotgunned half a face
and as the syphilitic paralysis
finally tagged him from behind he'd
close his one eye
remember '84
Providence
and conclude
his allotted
providence
must have been
exhausted during
that one glorious
season

PEE WEE REESE (1918–1999)   *inducted in 1984*

In LA

didn't have a choice back then
you went where they told you
or you didn't go at all
it was like the war all over again
you did your best but over it all
the stench of all the others
left behind

What Did We Expect

The umpire said I caught it
you deadpanned for fifty years
then
after you entered the Hall
leaving
the truth sealed
for ten years
ten long years
we waited
we hoped
we prayed
for you to finally kick
so we could read that
damn letter
and for
what

BRANCH RICKEY (1881–1965)   *inducted in 1967*

Steals

Friday
June 28
1907
the day
eight Senators
stole thirteen
bases
the last

day anyone
ever took
from you
something

you didn't
plan to
give away

Eppa Rixey

a Hollywood name
not a star's but a
veteran character
guy year after year
cast in horror shows
b(hind) movies
with lousy supporting
casts and bad direction
who still manages to
perform with distinction
equal to his name and
finally takes home his
Oscar

PHIL RIZZUTO (1917–) *inducted in 1994*

Holy Cow

Like most you've been hoodwinked by Scooter Rizzuto.
I've managed to see through the ruse.
I must now come forward, I can't remain mute. Oh,
please hear me! There's no time to lose!
I firmly believe that our great Constitution,
designed to divide church and state,
must now be invoked as a final solution,
and Congress cannot vacillate.
We should not permit him his bovine proclivities,
to mix up religion and games.
It's obvious he, through announcer activities,
has Hindu evangelist aims!
Beware! He's a vile, charismatic persuader.
I call on each Yank citizen:
Resist him with all of the courage you have or
we'll never eat burgers again!

Gopher

505 times
once a game
you watched as
they sauntered the
bases knowing they'd
won the battle yet
confident that you'd

Brooks Robinson (1937–)   *inducted in 1983*

Brooksie

had several affairs during his
career
remember the summer of '64
hard willowy ash blondes
each romance
fleeting and shaky
but
never struggled
with his third
tanned supple true
a perfect fit
the greatest of
marriages

Frank Robinson Was Never Loved

have to give to get
let them cheer for Brooks
mates and foes alike
got your message quick
true to given name
myopic pursuit
win the year's final game

JACKIE ROBINSON (1919–1972)   *inducted in 1962*

Forty-two's Chance

He looks TOO black — owners bristled
Whites will run scared — from bleachers

He's all muscle bound — Feller sure
Class C at best — no legitimacy

He's not chosen one — not before
Satch Josh Cool Papa — Negro deity

He don't worry me — Dixie whistled
Long as he ain't — no Dodger

He needed but one — Rickey provided
In taking his best — their worst

He whipped the darkness — so one-sided
Our cringing blanching NEED — the first

Uncle Robby Sat

a Brooklyn blue striped
Bhudda
watching Cardinal striped
Sunny Jim
fly past his Baltimore orange
ribbie record then
sighed and went back to sleep

Bullet

behind the plate
calls Satch's first pitch
ball one low
then the lazy curve
fouled back
and the 54 year old
knows he would've
PUNISHED that cripple
smiles inside
and fires his fabulous
famous no wind-up
three-quarters fastball
SMACK into his glove
and gives the one & one sign

Edd Roush's Twin

what the hell happened
inside mother
what special magic flowed
into him that I didn't get that
made him him
while I could only work that
goddamn farm my whole life
he even lived three weeks longer
than me the ornery s.o.b.

Red Ruffing at Seventeen

how could you know
losing four toes would
be your ticket out/in
while the crushing
coal black anguish
never vanished
your arm
carried you as far as
a man trading steel-toed boots
for a pair of toe-plated spikes
can go

Bait

As long as baseball's been around
debates continue unabated.
Trades: which one was most unsound
and which transaction should be fêted.
It seems the most lopsided deal
occurred in 1900 when
the Reds recalled the thunder peal
of Rusie's Hoosier arm from ten
years before and picked him up.
But all the lightning'd left ol' Amos,
a washed-up oh-and-one. The pup
they gave New York was Hall of Famous,
a hero with his fadeaway.
None have passed his NL wins,
the best of his or any day.
And yet the story's truth begins
with John T. Brush, the architect
of this Titanic of a swap.
For we can see, in retrospect,
just how the Giants reaped their crop.
While Brush owned Cincinnati outright,
the Giants soon would be his team.
He gave the Christy deal the green-light
then finished up his sneaky scheme.
You're sure this one's THE steal of steals?
You really should remind yourself
that when he made this worst of deals
John Brush was trading to himself!

Huggins's Babe

scolded and grounded
didn't mean to disappoint
I'll be good now Dad

The Night Before Nolan

'Twas the night before Nolan and through the hotel
Not a Blue Jay was sleeping. They weren't raising hell,
Or roosting at some pretty birdie's love nest.
Instead they all lay in their beds of unrest.

And why was Toronto in slumberless sorrow?
They knew Nolan Ryan was pitching tomorrow.
The batters all fretted and squirmed in their beds
While visions of oh-for-fours danced in their heads.

The next day, with psyches depressed and eyes bleary,
They all felt they'd rather commit hara-kiri.
When in to the clubhouse the manager strode,
His chance for a win heading down the commode.

"Wake up! Look alive," he implored with a bellow,
"The way you're all acting, I might think you're yellow!
"To think he's inspired this much immaturity:
"That old fart! He's ready for Social Security!"

The manager swooped and he squawked in their faces.
He even tried giving Lasorda embraces.
Soon they were cocky, their spirits aflame,
And he whistled, and shouted, and called them by name:

"Go Devo, go Alomar, Gruber and Carter!
"Go Olerud, Whiten, Glenallen, and Myers!
"And down in the nine spot, let's go, Manny Lee,
"Go score us some runs to support Jimmy Key!"

So out of the dugout those Blue Jays did fly
A sneer on their beaks and a gleam in each eye
"We'll take the old codger and rip him to bits.
"We'll pound Nolan Ryan, won't stop till he quits."

Two hours later they limped through the door,
Tailfeathers stomped, egos bruised to the core.
They didn't send Ryan's career up to heaven:
Instead he just tossed no-hit game number seven!

The Blue Jays knew nightmares and self-doubt would follow.
This bitter defeat would be so hard to swallow.
The silence was shattered as into the room
Walked Nolan, who said, "Hey boys, why all the gloom?"

"Go home. Get some rest. Heck, you know I can't play
Forever. Don't fret, I'll retire … someday!"
And they heard him exclaim as we laughed out of sight:
"Hey, thanks for the no-no, y'all have a good night!"

White

uniform worn clean
honored not for excellence
just for being good

RED SCHOENDIENST (1923–)   *inducted in 1989*

1974 Topps Card

with his
black and white
coaches in
black and white
his strawberry face pruned
from too many fungos
he was old like my granddad
but his card said he played
for nineteen years
shocked
a six year old first
feels the
melancholy
weight of
time

TOM SEAVER (1944–)   *inducted in 1992*

Please

lives a double life
for Mets fans his is
the twisted soul of a
dominatrix
pattern of pain and pleasure
degrading abandonment and sensuous
embrace
300 at home but for Sox
submissive voyeur hunger
and now the pure delicious anticipation
excruciating humiliation of Yankee games
helpless they pant for his
caress

FRANK SELEE (1859–1909)   *inducted in 1999*

Frank Selee Could See

what others couldn't   Frank Selee could see
foresight his vision   past weakness and pain
awkward catcher fumblings   through wracking scarred lungs
transformed into elegant scoops   deep in his inside game far inside
at first   the converging loci of poetry
slight flips from deep short he knew he would never see on the
revised as lightning   outside the game he saw far
dp pirouettes   far inside
peripheral coverage at third
adjusted with perfect clarity
in short order

Mr. No K

I didn't strike out
that's all anyone ever
talks about
hell I didn't just tap the
damn ball around
hit .312 almost 500 doubles
you know you have to hit it
out of the infield to get one
usually
even this lousy poet couldn't
come up with anything else

AL SIMMONS (1902–1956)   *inducted in 1953*

2927

Conlon photocloseups
19 with freckles and an
unlined confidence I can
hit anybody with or without
a bat
37 going on ancient
freckles dissolved
into late night creases
white temples the ignored omen
that 3000 should have but would never
come

George Sisler and Son

the kid follows
and fails of course
as a star
   monstrous shoes can
   never fit again so perfectly
yet with one magic stroke
exceeds the father
as a teammate
   and the father thrills with
   pride and the tiniest twinge
   of green series envy

ENOS SLAUGHTER (1916–)   *inducted in 1985*

Be Careful What You Wish For

you got it all wrong
the whiny campaign
got you in but now
you're just another
one of many who
lower the standards
and nobody thinks
of you anymore

Satch's Caddie

Trudging in from the pen
AGAIN awash in Satch's
applause he can hardly
believe he's gone from star
to shadow so fast and while the
Pitchin' Man gets a straight
15 percent off the top there's still
66 percent of game left in his lap but
what can you do but bust Number
One a little harder and snap the
Deuce a little sharper and prove
that brightest isn't necessarily
best

Home

well
what did you
expect
your name spelled out
hero
but even it was only third best
centerfielder name in the city
it was all a different world
to you a baffling swirl of
weighty expectation
unfulfilled
finally your coastal
emancipation came
but
of course
being a ballplayer
you hadn't read
Thomas Wolfe

WARREN SPAHN (1921–)   *inducted in 1973*

Swing and a Woof

perpetually mourning
Basset hound face
the same old southpaw but
when the old ones still work
who needs new tricks

ALBERT SPALDING (1850–1915)   *inducted in 1939*

Goodwill My Butt

all he ever owned
owed to America's Game
capitalism

TRIS SPEAKER (1888–1958)   *inducted in 1937*

Every Time Tris Speaker

spoke
to Cobb
    in private
    in the dugout
    in Shibe
    in '28
or goofed an easy one
or left them loaded
or got nailed at second

he wondered
if they wondered

Pop Music

I never loved you
too big too strong
too slow too scary
They made you
captain after my
Roberto was gone
but it didn't work
with me
Then the fam-a-lee
crap started and I
was a disco-hater
But your vintage windmill
your cap worn stars
wore me down like a
hypnotic rhythm by game
seven
until I became part of the
We and while disco will
forever suck I love that
song

Detroit Stars

Briggs gazed down at his
army of ants as they each
worked their individually
insignificant task that
added up to cars in the lot
and cash in his pocket and
picked out one

He watched as that black ant
placed the hook in the ring
over and over and over and
thought what a waste while
dreaming of a white Turkey
roaming free in center for his
Tigers

Think of how he could gobble
up flies he chuckled aloud
then shook his head at the
folly and shifted right to a
Thanksgiving dream with all
the trimmings plus breast meat
just the breast meat

And the hook goes in the ring
and the hook goes in the ring
and the hook goes in the ring

Casey at the Table (The Battle of the Republic)

The outlook wasn't brilliant for the year of '94:
The owners and the players had begun their greedy war.
And when the season's cancellation seemed to be their aim,
A sickly feeling fell upon the patrons of the game.

The fans were tired of all the talk and rhetoric from Fehr,
And ev'ry time that Ravitch spoke he proved a horse's rear.
"Why can't they simply find a way to split their billion bucks?"
The fans would ask themselves, then say to one another, "Shucks!"

"The season was the most exciting seen in quite a while.
Denying us the chase of Maris' record: Why, it's vile!
And Gwynn was gonna hit .400! What a thrilling scene!
If only by some miracle a Saint would intervene."

"The Expos and the Braves were set to fight until the finish.
The Indians, for goodness' sakes, were looking rather winnish.
And though the AL West was bad, the season (till it ceased)
Could hold our int'rest long enough to see who stunk the least."

But no, the Lords of Baseball and the Union had decided
To stop the game and all the joy and magic it provided.
There was a chance there wouldn't be a Series played that year,
A situation guaranteed to conjure up a tear.

A few forgot about the game entirely. The rest
Clung to that hope which "springs eternal in the human breast";
"A miracle! An angel sent to help us from on high!
Oh Lord, we do beseech Thee!" was the fans' impassioned cry.

Then from the heavens up above there came a funny sound.
It chuckled through the valley; and it laughed along the ground.
It filled the stands with merriment and goosed the fans with mirth,
For Casey, Casey Stengel, was descending to the earth.

The fans could not believe their eyes, because "The Old Perfesser,"
Dressed up in his angelic garb resembled a cross-dresser!
But when a closer look revealed that craggy, wrinkled face,
A Mets cap perched upon his head; it had to be "Ol' Case."

"I've been discharged from there, and now I'm here in present time.
And strange enough us Angels have to speak on earth in rhyme.
And though I never played for them while I was just a pup
Because of course they weren't a team and you could look it up."

"But like I said I've been discharged again without a choice.
The Boss (not George) felt I should be the diplomatic voice.
I'm set to figure out this mess, get to the nitty gritty
Like when I straightened out that Senatudinal Committee."

So off he went to try to put an end to all the pain.
The sight was just Amazin': Casey flew without a plane!
The hopes were that, with talks that had been anything but stable,
Negotiations would improve with Casey at the table.

There was ease in Casey's manner as he glided to the place.
There was light round Casey's halo and a glow about his face.
And when, to greet the quibblers, he lightly doffed his cap,
A bird flew out! There was no doubt: Ol' Casey was the chap

Who'd smile with Christian charity: he'd bid the game continue.
He'd try with ev'ry saintly bone, with each cherubic sinew.
However, both the lawyers scowled at Casey with disdain.
The optimism of the fans had now begun to wane.

For though St. Casey came to them to help negotiation,
In fact they never cared about the game's annihilation.
With pockets lined with cash it was an option they could choose.
Could Casey make them understand that ev'ryone would lose?

The smile is gone from Casey's face; instead, determination.
Indeed, the time for clowning's gone, replaced by consternation.
And now he floats into the room and now he shuts the door.
And now one question still remains: Could Casey halt the war?

Oh! somewhere major leaguers play because they love the game.
The owners act responsibly, not seeking those to blame.
The nation gets its Pastime back, and fans can cheer and shout.
But there is no joy in baseball — even Casey has struck out.

DON SUTTON (1945–)   *inducted in 1998*

Scuff

a never ending series of
sixteen and elevens and
seventeen and thirteens
never
Sutton's pitching tonight
let's get tickets
never
oh no not Sutton again we're
screwed
never
ace except maybe as a hardware
man what grade sandpaper do
you need how about thumbtacks
of course we've got thumbtacks
but he dragged it out there every fifth
day winlosswinlosswinwinloss
until he finally hung up his tool belt
and defied us to lock him out

BILL TERRY (1898–1989)   *inducted in 1954*

Job

hell no it wasn't fun and games
work isn't supposed to be is it
it was a roof and three squares
every out and every damn loss
another shirt stolen off my back
I had to climb a goddamn mountain
every year just to make a living
but no s.o.b. was gonna keep me
from getting what was coming to
me
and my kids

Sam vs The Press

got ripped in the papers for
hitting homers
    the least difficult
    of hits as it requires
    only muscle and not
    brains to make it
Sam said let one of them try
to hit one out and a century
later the s.o.b.'s still can't

JOE TINKER (1880–1948)   *inducted in 1946*

The Power of the Pen

For many men considered Hall of Famers,
their worthiness was obvious. But Tinker?
His case inspired multiple disclaimers
from those who made that vote: "I'm not a drinker!"
Compared to all the others judged immortal,
the shifting sands of history will show it.
His puny stats can force a man to chortle.
He only made it in by word of poet.

Pie Who

i got my richie hebner model
glove and bat and a helmet all
with number 20 on it with black
magic marker and my pirates t
shirt with 20 on the back so
how come he can't wear
20
anymore

a pie trainer

who

so what if he's dead
i never heard of him

what's richie now

3

dad
i need a new pirates shirt and a
new richie hebner glove and a new

DAZZY VANCE (1891–1961)   *inducted in 1955*

Inspiration

the accountant reads
he didn't stick until he
was 31 and still won 197
could there be time he
hopes as he finds his
glove buried deep in the garage
and with an accountant's
realistic sensibilities rotates his
arm grips the scuffed green
dream on frayed red laces
with
   his
      knuckles

ARKY VAUGHAN (1912–1952)   *inducted in 1985*

Quietly He Slipped Beneath

never needed help
before and would
just as soon have kept it
that way but even
silent wheels no
matter how perfectly
shaped still
sometimes
rust

Just a Five Year Break

Christ, the man's the anti–Christ!
He must be stopped at any cost,
and if we fail, all hope is lost.
Our game will fall to pieces.

I tell you, he's Beelzebub!
His open collar mocking us,
without a doubt, an incubus
whose influence increases.

Of course he is the Lord of Flies!
I'll bet his only foot is cloven.
Remember all the schemes he's woven,
his evil masterpieces?

Who else but Lucifer could send
a midget to the plate? I ask
each one of you to take this task
before our power ceases.

The Prince of Darkness owns the Browns.
It's clear we need an exorcist.
We simply cannot coexist
with all his vile caprices.

Baseball's Satan's finally gone!
But still we can't repeat our sin
of letting shysters like him in:
those Mephistopheleses.

Never

couldn't happen today God's gift buried under
    prescription mountains
    harnessed conformity
    starved expectations

he'd never get near a chance not even as a
    fireman

HONUS WAGNER (1874–1955)   *inducted in 1936*

Honus

sat in the car and
weakly waved as they
pulled the string then
as they drove away

stood forever hard and
tall and proud
watching Maz's
shot bounce close

dragged from mapled
shade to the bleached
concrete sea of Gate C
unmistakable roar of
Series wins washing over

stirred as another broke the
long lonely silence and asked
Roberto why he just had to play
that last inning
that last game
that last season
to break his mark
then cracked a rusty smile

BOBBY WALLACE (1873–1960)   *inducted in 1953*

Loser's Limerick

This shortstop turned manager Wallace:
His records will never enthrall us.
His team would get smeared,
Yet he still was Revered
Although he lost more than Cornwallis!

ED WALSH (1881–1959)   *inducted in 1946*

Before He Pitched

awoke screaming from
the deafening roar
of swishing limp bats
balls into mitts
asses onto benches
the pressure squeezing
inning after inning
batter after batter
pitch after pitch
knowing that perfection
might yet again be
necessary

Leadoff

back home in Harrah which
by the way is spelled Harrah
backwards there was always
some work needin' doin' and
ever since I can remember it
was my job to set the table
everyday and seein' as Paul
an' me were gonna be together
up north anyway I didn't see
any reason not to just keep on
doin' my job

PAUL WANER (1903–1965) *inducted in 1952*

Paul Waner on Life

shoot for the lines you said
either it's a double or you're
still swinging but geez most of
us are lucky just to get a piece
of it and would gladly settle for
the medium deep fly to center
and get the hell outta there
cripes some need a good stiff
drink just to find legs enough to
step to the plate but then you sure
didn't have a problem there either
so what we need to know is when
the chalk dust settled for good was
it all as easy
for you
as it isn't
for us

John Montgomery Ward's Plaque

fails to mention his Players' League
a grave injustice that still stirs the fight
in him raising his Elysian
(and not Hoboken either)
appearance every night in the Hall of
Immortals an eternal one-sided debate
raging at bronze busts of Ban
Johnson and Spalding with ballgame
ferocity for a defense that will never
rest until his appeal for recasting
is granted

Pastime

examines every seed with
magnifier meticulousness
charts growth/fertilizer
        correlations
ponders plot shifts and
        crop rotations
        rages against insects
        rodents and weather
even turns his sun hat backwards
and screams at the root rot but
it's just not the same

GM

born poor German and oompah
tuba fat every contract
a series game you
struck out DiMaggio and Mantle
homered off Whitey and threw
Scooter and Billy out at the plate
and with each
victory your raised arms quickly
dove
into deep pockets adding green
to glorious Yankee green

SMILING MICKEY WELCH (1859–1941)   *inducted in 1973*

Gone

your buddies gone to
  the Players' League
your arm gone too
your last shot but
  as each shot rang out and
  they whirled around you in
your squared box
your nickname slowly leaked from
your face when you found it wasn't
your box anymore never to be
your box again

The Devil in Veracruz

Willie Wells in Mexico
was so much more than
Willie Wells in Chicago or
St. Louis or Newark and
it wasn't the weather or
the lousy pitching or the
margaritas or even the
señoritas it was much
simpler than that so
damned simple

>   In Mexico
>   The Devil
>   was
>   a man

>   Back home
>   the man
>   was
>   a devil

Enough to
sing the blues
playin' for the Blues

The Demise of a Brooklyn God

eyes clear
wrists snappy
arm loaded
knees fluid
        but
those tiny
size sevens
shredded support
the ankles
your achilles

…and he
became the chaff…

Hoyt Wilhelm (1923–)   *inducted in 1985*

Hoyt Wilhelm Pitched

1070 times
more than all but
Orosco yet despite his
shiny red hero helmet
all those fires doused
he rocks himself
to sleep not with k's or w's
but that sweet solid first pitch
first swing first kiss
first and last
dinger

B. Williams If

his way not an open road
romance but
whirring drone of steely framed
hardware
thick chrome plate effort
repeated
the family wagon that always
made it home
parked out in left full tank ready
to drive

SMOKEY JOE WILLIAMS (1886–1951)   *inducted in 1999*

Remember

1946 tending in Harlem
through the yellow haze
and bourbon talk turns to
who's the best ever and
while some say Cy some
Big Train someone mentions
him without realizing

    embers begin to
    glow faintly like a
    cigarette drag
    at dusk

but then Satch comes up and
the tales spill across the bar
mixing with the beer nuts and
laughter

    and the thin
    gray wisps
    drift silently
    into oblivion

What about you Joe they ask
but he just shakes his silver
head and pours himself another
double

TED WILLIAMS (1918–)   *inducted in 1966*

Splintered

distilled American
singular stud
master of sticks
ash
reel or
flight control
alone not lonely in
box
stream or
miles high

now
wheeled like a '70s
reliever
never left
yet so

alone

VIC WILLIS (1876–1947)   *inducted in 1995*

Who Was Vic Willis

once bright and clear
strong enough to lose
29 and be COVETED
like a sunned photo you
quickly faded from Pgh.
to St.L. to vanished and
even your own day in the
bronzy spotlight can't
illuminate the bleached
memory of your brilliance

Hack Wilson and Friends

pony bottle Babe
with more big Chicago
hits
than Capone
trinity created just for
their time and place their
lives a lusty roar followed
close by hoarse shrunken
whisper until
within months of each other
the party was over

DAVE WINFIELD (1951–) *inducted in 2001*

Monster

So long we watched waiting
waiting for Mr. Three Sport
to finally fill those size
seventeen spikes but
hell only MONSTER will cut it
when you're batting stance
spreads from coast to coast so
that faint Mr. May halitosis
lingered
until a seven hop double up
North turned him into King
David and what I can't fathom
is how after twenty years of
just not quite good enough
Goliath can sneak up on you

GEORGE WRIGHT (1847–1937)   *inducted in 1937*
HARRY WRIGHT (1835–1895)   *inducted in 1953*

Brothers in 5/4

Never good enough
I was the best
Threw with either hand
Scored five a game
But still he rode me
With subtle whip
A glance or the lack
Subconscious war
Proving he was boss
Always the boss
Why did pro ball's
Father
Have to be my
Brother

Wouldn't hold his hand
He was a man
Taught him all he knew
Made him a star
But was he grateful
Hell I paid him
Even more than me
Pouted instead
I only gave him
What we needed
To win I must
Father
We lose if I'm
Brother

EARLY WYNN (1920–1999)   *inducted in 1972*

At 299

late in '62
cursed the gods for not granting
one more of his name

CARL YASTRZEMSKI (1939–)   *inducted in 1989*

Yaz on LIFE

captured in still life
running no fleeing
strain no terror
to be merely out
or did you see all
the big final outs of your
future
67 75 78 67 75 78 67 75 78
numbers hunting you
between the bases like
radar
did you realize this stretch
drive overdrive high octane
performance would be it for you
your clutch forever after
worn out

TOM YAWKEY (1903–1976)   *inducted in 1980*

Windmills

Steinbrenner with a big tilted heart
He hacked away at his
Monster everyday
Desperate for that one
Conquering blow but the
Louisville sword the continuous
flow of green could never complete
The Impossible Dream

CY YOUNG (1867–1955)   *inducted in 1937*

First Last and Always

all those summers
in the big cities
all those dollars
big league salaries still
the smell of molasses
corn husks freshly
turned Ohio sod
cow patties never left
first last and always
a rube from the sticks
sophistication and guile
saved for the simple
square of the strike zone

S Is for

forever Young and a Giant
in the boxscores
all run through fence football
desire like Muggsy loved
as if each game were his last
eventually true for all of us
perhaps his missing letter a
subconscious message to him

Soon

Robin Yount (1955–)   *inducted in 1999*

Robin Yount Was Never

About the records even when they were so
Sure he'd break them all just look at his hits
Before twenty-five but Robin Yount was never

Certain of anything in baseball only that it
Was hard work and hard to win and so very
Very hard to lose still Robin Yount was never

Gonna let them run his life not with so much of it
To live so there was some Harley mischief and
Approach shots although Robin Yount was never

Anything but a ballplayer so when the SS shoulder
Finally gave out and they asked him to move to
Center you better believe Robin Yount was never

Half-assed about anything so he became an MVP
And marched past 3000 a young man with a legit
Shot at four but Robin Yount was never ever

A Pete Rose except in nickname Charlie so when it
Was time he knew then silhouetted jumped a mound
Into the auburn Colorado sky high as a sand wedge

Index of Titles and First Lines